microQuests

daring
cell
defenders

WITHDRAWN

Rebecca L. Johnson

illustrations by Jack Desrocher
diagrams by Jennifer E. Fairman, CMI

M Millbrook Press • Minneapolis

For Eric Channing Wood—RLJ

Many of the photographs in this book are micrographs. Micrographs are photos taken through a microscope. Sometimes bright colors are added to micrographs to make cell parts easier to see. Other times, cells are stained with dye so cells and cell structures show up more clearly under a microscope.

As you read this book, look for the bold words in colored boxes. These words tell you about the photos and diagrams. You can also look for the lines that connect the photos and the text.

Millbrook Press, Inc.
A division of Lerner Publishing Group, Inc.
241 First Avenue North
Minneapolis, MN 55401 U.S.A.

Website address: www.lernerbooks.com

Library of Congress Cataloging-in-Publication Data

Johnson, Rebecca L.
    Daring cell defenders / by Rebecca L. Johnson ; illustrated by Jack Desrocher and Jennifer E. Fairman.
        p. cm. – (Microquests)
    Includes index.
    ISBN 978-0-8225-7140-7 (lib. bdg. : alk. paper)
    1. Immune system—Juvenile literature.   2. Cellular immunity—Juvenile literature.
3. Allergy—Juvenile literature.   I. Desrocher, Jack.   II. Fairman, Jennifer E.   III. Title.
QR181.8.J64 2008
616.07'9—dc22   2007001427

Manufactured in the United States of America
1 2 3 4 5 6 – DP – 13 12 11 10 09 08

table of contents

chapter 1
invisible invaders

Imagine a castle. Its stone walls are solid and strong. Inside those walls, all is snug and safe.

Then one day, an alarm rings out. The castle is under attack! Invaders have broken open the gate!

From every corner of the castle, defenders appear. They're a tough-looking bunch. Both sides draw their weapons, and the battle begins. For a while, it looks like the invaders might win. But the defenders do not give up. The last invader falls. The war is won, and the castle is saved!

Now imagine the castle is your body. Like a castle, your body is built to keep out invaders. It's well defended too.

Instead of stones, though, your body is made of cells. Cells are the smallest units of life. They are the building blocks of all living things. Single cells are so small you can see them only with a microscope. Your body is made up of about 100 trillion cells.

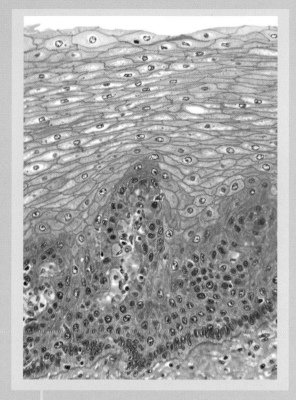

Groups of cells working together form tissues. Groups of tissues form organs like your heart, lungs, and brain. Groups of organs, in turn, join forces to make up body systems. For example, your heart, blood vessels, and blood form your circulatory system.

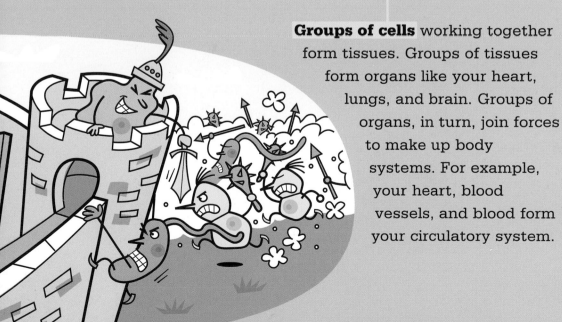

The world outside your body is filled with all sorts of cells. Many are harmless. But others are up to no good. If harmful cells get inside your body, they can make you sick. People often call these harmful cells germs.

Some germs are bacteria. (Just one is called a bacterium.) Bacteria are one-celled living things. Some are round. Others are straight like rods or twisted into spiral shapes. Most are about one hundredth the size of your smallest cell. Bacteria make copies of themselves by dividing over and over again. Bacteria can multiply very quickly. Just a few can become millions overnight.

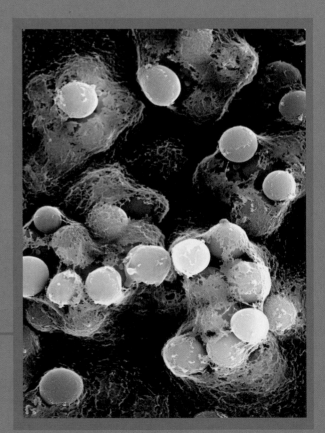

Not all bacteria are bad. Some very good ones live in your intestines. They help you get the most from the food you digest. But other bacteria cause serious diseases such as pneumonia and whooping cough. Still **others cause illnesses like strep throat** and diarrhea.

Viruses are the tiniest of all body invaders. They are far smaller than bacteria. Viruses aren't actually cells. Technically, they're not even alive.

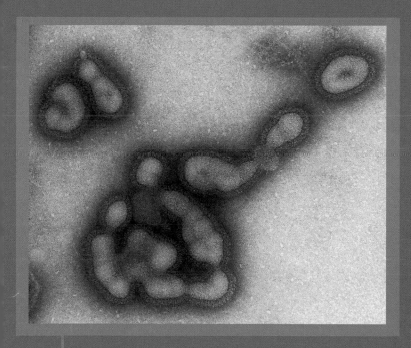

When viruses invade your body, they take over some of your cells. They turn those cells into little factories that make more viruses. Those viruses go on to invade more cells. Those cells churn out even more viruses. On and on, the cycle goes.

Being invaded by viruses can mean getting diseases such as chicken pox and colds. **Viruses cause flu** and cold sores too.

You can't escape germs. Bacteria and viruses are everywhere around you. They're in the air you breathe. They're in the food you eat. They're **on your skin** and everything you touch.

No matter where you go or what you do, germs are all around. If they get a chance to invade your body, they will. An invasion by germs is called an infection.

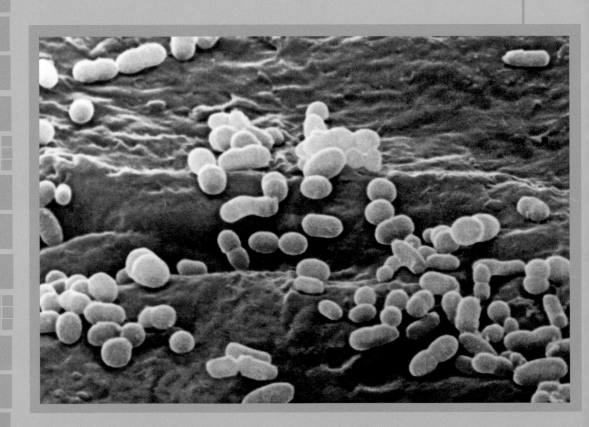

When germs cause an infection, special cells inside your body come to the rescue. These cell defenders are constantly on guard against bacteria, viruses, and other intruders. They will track down and destroy anything that might do you harm.

These cell defenders, together with cells that keep invaders out, form your immune system. That's the body system that fights infection and disease. When you get sick or injured, your immune system helps you get well.

chapter 2

body barriers

Keeping foreign invaders out of your body is a big job. So it's not surprising that your biggest organ plays a role.

That organ is your skin. Think of skin as body armor. It protects what lies beneath it. But unlike the armor worn by knights who guarded castles, skin can stretch!

Your skin is made up of about 300 million skin cells. They are packed tightly together. They form a strong, stretchy, waterproof barrier between you and the outside world. As long as it's not cut or torn, skin keeps germs on the outside from getting in.

Of course, not every inch of you is covered by skin. Your body has a few openings, like your mouth, nose, and eyes. You need these openings to eat, breathe, and see. But any opening is like a door. It's a way for germs to enter.

That's why these body openings are well guarded. Take your eyes, for instance. Every few seconds, you blink. Each time your eyelids close, they cover your eyeball with tears. Tears are salty. They also contain a substance that kills bacteria. **Blinking** keeps your eyes clean. Germs that get into them are usually washed away before they can get into your body. Getting dust or larger particles in your eyes may even make you cry. Flooding the eyes with tears helps remove anything that might scratch them and create a way in for germs.

The inside of your mouth is always wet. Some of this wetness is saliva. Saliva is made by special groups of cells in your mouth. These cell groups are called glands. As you chew, saliva starts breaking down your food. Saliva also kills bacteria.

Many cells that line your mouth make thick, clear liquid called mucus. Germs that enter your mouth get caught in this slimy stuff.

Cells at the back of your mouth and in your throat have tiny bristles called cilia. **Cilia** beat back and forth like miniature brooms. They sweep up invaders that get trapped in mucus. When you clear your throat and swallow, those germs end up in your stomach. Powerful chemicals in your stomach kill them.

Tiny hairs grow just inside your nose. They catch some of the germs you breathe in. Cells that line your nose produce mucus. If germs make it past the hairs, they usually get stuck in mucus.

Cells lining your nose have cilia too. These move trapped germs away. Some germs get swept downward. You get rid of them when you blow your nose. Others are swept into your throat, to be coughed out or swallowed.

Mucus, saliva, cilia, and skin form your body's first line of defense against germs. Sometimes invaders get past these barriers. But your body has other ways to fight those germs.

first responder cells

Let's say you're outside, playing fetch with your dog. You toss an old, dirty stick. He brings it back. On the next throw, you feel a sharp pain in your hand. A sliver of wood is stuck deep in your palm.

A sliver might not seem like a big deal. But something important has happened. Your skin barrier has been broken. Bacteria were living in the dirt on the stick. They have just entered your body.

Inside your palm, the **bacteria begin to divide**. A few turn into dozens. Dozens become hundreds. The bacteria release poisons called toxins. Toxins begin to kill body cells around the wound.

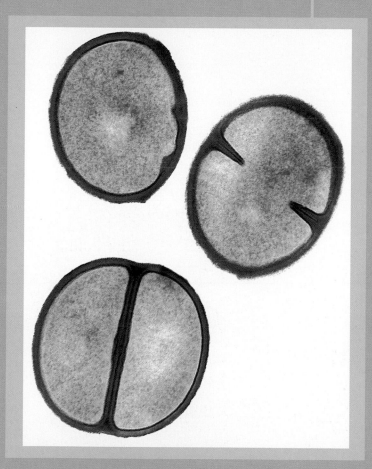

But cell defenders are already on their way. They come from your blood. Blood has both red and white blood cells. The red cells carry oxygen—a gas—to all body cells. White blood cells are part of the immune system. Neutrophils are one type of white blood cell. Moving along with blood, neutrophils patrol your entire body. They're always watching out for trouble.

When the splinter poked into your skin, damaged skin cells released chemicals. These chemicals are like an alarm going off. Neutrophils passing close to the wound sense this chemical alarm. Instantly, they go into action.

The neutrophils flatten out and **squeeze between cells** that form blood vessel walls. They move out of the blood and head for the bacteria around the wound. A cell war has begun!

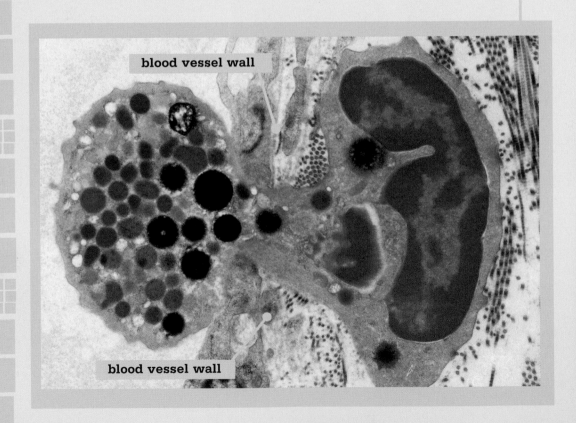

blood vessel wall

blood vessel wall

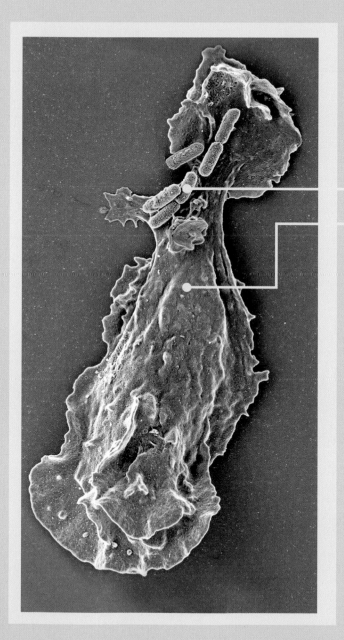

Neutrophils look like they are full of dots. The dots are little sacs packed with powerful chemicals. The chemicals can dissolve **bacteria**.

Each **neutrophil** targets one bacterium. When defender and invader are nearly touching, the neutrophil curves out and around the bacterium. In a flash, it "swallows" the bacterium whole. Like tiny bombs, the neutrophil's chemical weapons explode. The captured bacterium begins to dissolve.

The neutrophil dies too. But hundreds more are arriving every second. Your bones make billions of neutrophils every day. Even if they aren't attacking invaders, they live only a few days.

More and more neutrophils arrive. They kill bacteria one by one. But the bacteria divide faster and faster. Some bacteria move away from the wound. The infection is spreading.

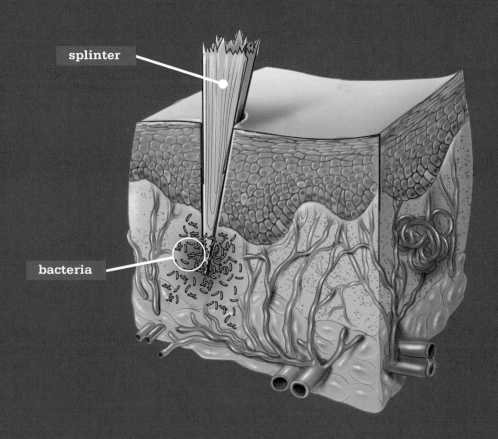

splinter

bacteria

Fortunately, new defenders arrive. Meet the macrophages. These invader-eaters are your largest white blood cells.

You have lots of **macrophages** in parts of your body that are

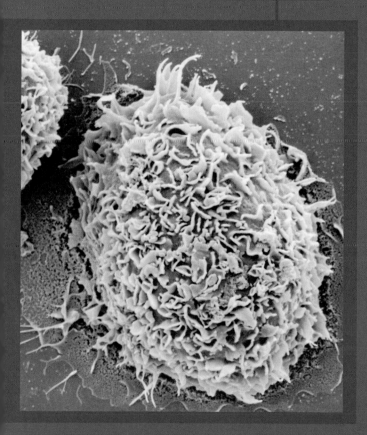

especially open to attack. Macrophages in your lungs are ready to snare invaders you breathe in. Other teams of macrophages live in your liver, kidneys, and brain.

Huge numbers of macrophages also roam through your body on the lookout for threats. They mostly travel in blood, like neutrophils. Macrophages can also squeeze between cells that form blood vessel walls to attack invaders.

Macrophages can eat more than neutrophils. A single macrophage can swallow about one hundred bacteria.

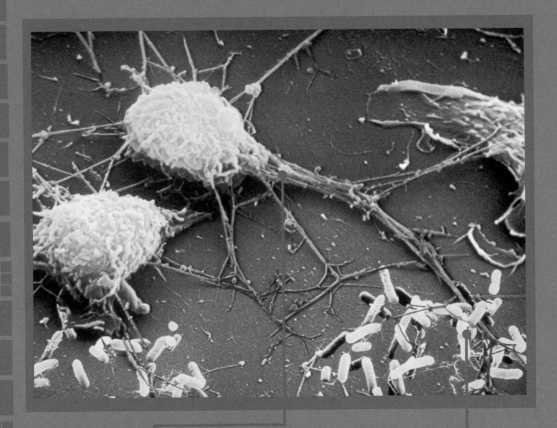

As a macrophage closes in for the kill, it changes shape. **Armlike extensions** grow out from it. They grip **bacteria** and pull them inside the big cell.

Macrophages also release a special chemical that works like a signal flare. It attracts more macrophages and neutrophils to the battle zone.

The chemical serves another purpose too. Together with other substances in blood, it triggers inflammation. The infected area becomes swollen, red, and hot. It starts to hurt too.

Inflammation helps cell defenders do their job. It increases the amount of blood flowing to the wound. This brings more white blood cells to the scene. Cells that form the walls of blood vessels also shrink. This makes it easier for macrophages and neutrophils to slip between them.

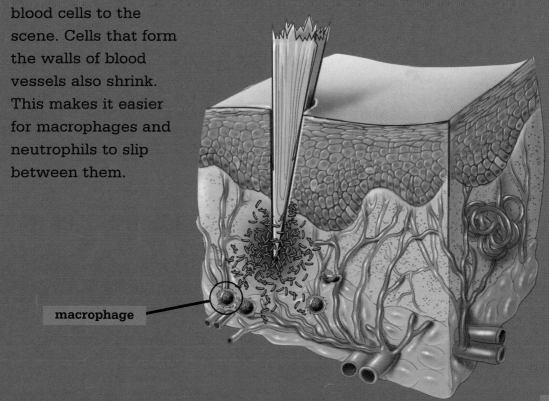

macrophage

In a serious infection, the chemical macrophages make also causes fever. When you have a fever, your body's temperature goes up. Most people's normal body temperature is around 98°F (37°C). Fever can raise that temperature by several degrees.

At a higher temperature, cell defenders move faster. They also gobble up bacteria with greater speed. But the heat slows down bacteria. Fever helps the defenders get ahead.

Around the sliver, the battle rages on. Bacteria keep dividing. They pump out more toxins. The defenders keep on fighting. They gobble up bacteria as fast as they can.

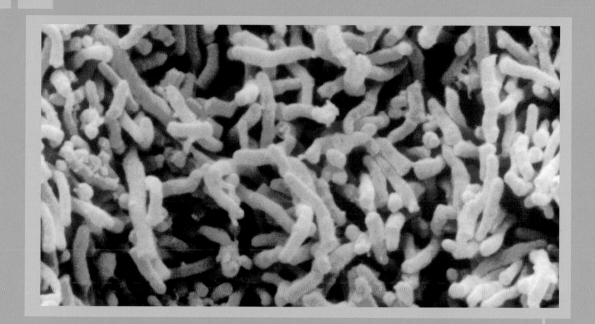

After several hours, many bacteria and white blood cells have died. The area around the splinter is packed with their remains. This gooey white stuff is **pus**. Pus usually forms in infected wounds. It's inside pimples too. Pus is made up of dead white blood cells and the bacteria they've killed.

Bacteria are dying, but the invading army is still very strong. And now a few bacteria have escaped into blood vessels. Traveling in the blood, they are moving around in your body. If some of these traveling bacteria attack cells somewhere else, they could start another infection. Or they might break into cells, hide out for a while, and cause an infection later. Either way, it's time to call in the big guns.

chapter 4

hunting down the enemy

Just as things are looking serious, another type of white blood cell arrives. These cells are not as big as macrophages. They have no tiny bombs, like neutrophils. They don't gobble up invaders. Yet these cells are probably the most powerful defenders you have. They are lymphocytes.

Macrophages and neutrophils have carried out the first part of the attack. Lymphocytes will handle the second part. They have weapons that will help your body win the war against the invaders.

Lymphocytes come in several forms. The ones that just arrived on the scene are helper T lymphocytes. They're often called helper T cells.

When helper T cells arrive, they head for macrophages. The macrophages have placed pieces of the enemy on their cell membranes. (The cell membrane is a cell's outer covering.) The pieces are chemicals called proteins.

Macrophages wear these enemy proteins like badges. But they're not for show. These protein badges let macrophages and lymphocytes communicate.

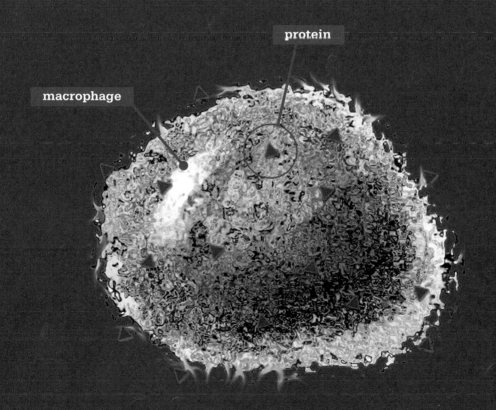

protein

macrophage

A helper T cell approaches a macrophage. It locks onto one of the enemy proteins on the macrophage's surface.

Then the lymphocyte "memorizes" that protein. The helper T cell now knows exactly what the enemy looks like—chemically, at least. The helper T cell will use that information to start the next phase of the war.

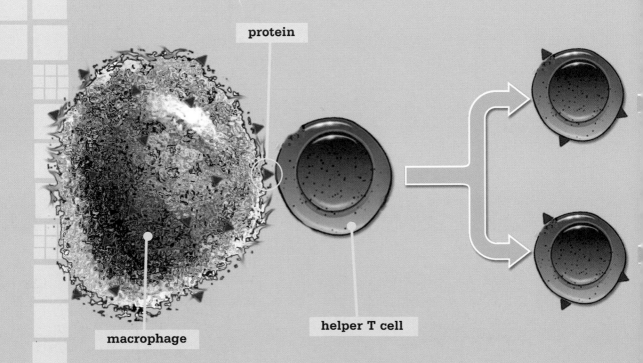

protein

macrophage

helper T cell

To carry out its mission, the helper T cell begins to divide. One cell becomes two. Those two become four, eight, sixteen, and so on. Every new cell has the same information about the enemy as the original cell.

These new helper T cells move out into the body. They will tell other parts of the immune system about the enemy.

Some of the helper T cells go in search of killer T cells. Killer T cells are another kind of lymphocyte. As you might guess from the name, they're especially deadly.

When **helper T cells** meet **killer T cells**, they share information about the invading bacteria's proteins. They program killer T cells to destroy any **body cell** in which invading bacteria might be hiding.

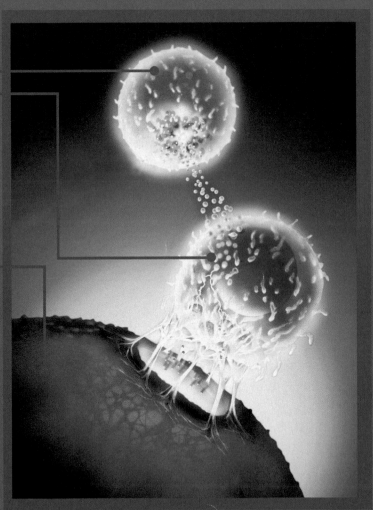

The killer T cells head out to track down these undercover enemies. Wherever they encounter body cells with invading bacteria inside them, they move in for the kill.

But there are still plenty of bacteria out in the open. Helper T cells deal with this problem too. They meet up with still another kind of lymphocyte. They are B lymphocytes, or B cells. The B cells know some special tricks.

armed with antibodies

At first glance, B cells and T cells look much alike. But B cells are the source of your immune system's secret weapon.

Helper T cells pass chemical information about the enemy to B cells. Those B cells divide again and again. A team of identical B cells is formed. Almost immediately, the team of B cells starts producing proteins called antibodies.

B cells can make many different kinds of antibodies. Each kind of **antibody** defends against one particular kind of invader,

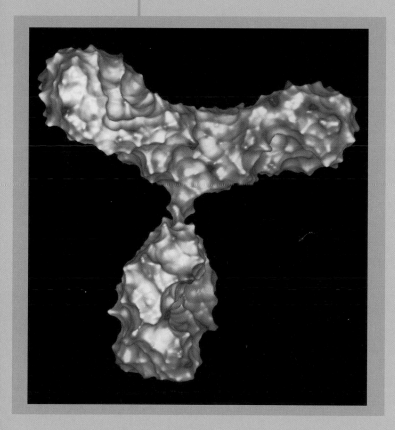

such as the bacteria that entered through the wound in your hand.

B cells release antibodies into your blood. They also release them into the fluid that surrounds body cells. The result is millions of enemy-tracking antibodies on the move throughout your body.

When antibodies find an enemy bacterium, they attach to its surface. In the blink of an eye, the enemy is covered with antibodies.

Antibodies fight invaders in two ways. First, they turn the bacteria they've attached to into targets. Macrophages and neutrophils chase down these antibody-coated targets. The bacteria don't have a chance. The white blood cells devour them.

With help from chemicals in blood, antibodies also cause holes to form in bacteria's cell membranes. The holes let the bacteria's insides leak out. The enemy cells collapse.

neutrophil

macrophage

antibody

bacterium

Soon your blood is packed with millions and millions of antibodies. The invading bacteria are no match for this secret weapon. The tide of the battle turns. The bacteria are slowly but surely destroyed. Your daring cell defenders have won.

At the site where the splinter entered your palm, the inflammation decreases. The pus around the sliver presses against it. The pressure pushes the sliver back up through the skin. The sliver may pop out entirely, along with some of the pus.

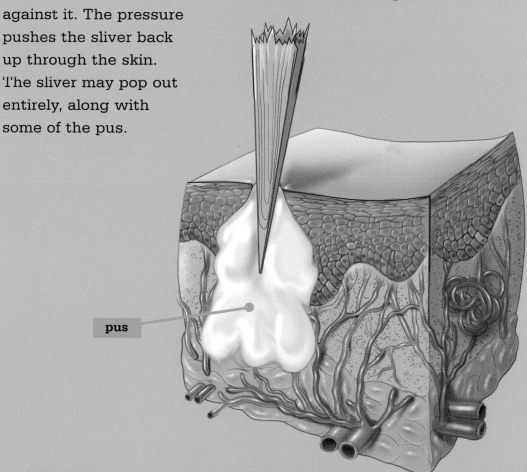

pus

When the bacteria are dead and the sliver is gone, the **wound heals**. New skin cells grow to replace those that died. After a few days, your skin is completely repaired.

The cell defenders don't all go away after winning the war. Killer T cells continue their patrol. They look for any invaders that might still be in hiding somewhere.

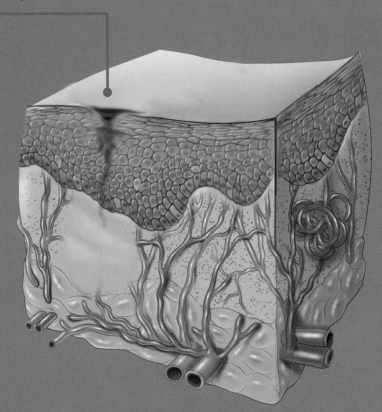

The specially programmed B cells stop making the antibodies that defeated this enemy. With the bacteria wiped out, your body doesn't need that particular weapon anymore.

Over time, most of the members of this B cell team will die out. But a few will remain. They will stay with you for the rest of your life.

chapter 6
cells with long memories

The B cell soldiers that live on after the war won't ever forget the enemy they defeated. For that reason, they're called memory B cells.

If the same bacteria invade you again, the memory B cells will spring into action. They'll start making the antibodies you need to fight that particular enemy right away. Your body will win the war much more quickly the second time.

Memory B cells give you immunity. Immunity means being safe (or at least safer) from germs that have attacked you before.

You develop immunity when germs invade your body. Those germs might enter through a break in the skin, like those on a sliver. Or they might invade another part of your body to cause a disease.

Take a disease like measles. **Measles is caused by a virus.** You might breathe it in. It could also invade if you had measles virus on your fingers and then touched your mouth or nose.

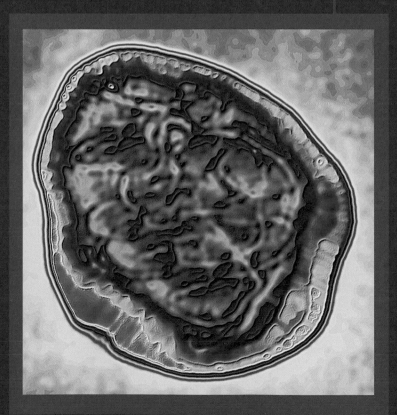

Measles viruses usually attack cells in the back of the throat. Like other viruses, they take over the cells they infect. The viruses force the cells to make more viruses that go on to infect more cells. Soon cells in the lungs and all over the skin are infected too.

The viruses release toxins into the body. People with measles can get really sick, with a cough and high fever. A blotchy red rash appears all over their body.

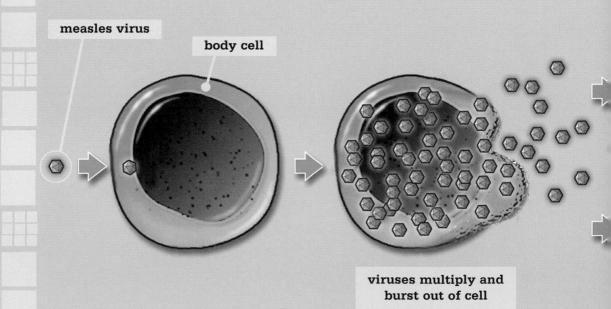

measles virus

body cell

viruses multiply and
burst out of cell

But the body's cell defenders fight back. Killer T cells form. They hunt down measles viruses hiding inside body cells. A new team of B cells forms too. They make antibodies that stick to measles viruses and help destroy them.

After a week or two, the immune system usually wins. The cell defenders defeat the virus. The person gradually gets well.

Thanks to immunity, a person who has had measles probably will never get it again. Some of the B cells that made measles antibodies will live on in the person's body. If the measles virus attacks again, those cells will take action right away. The virus will be killed before it has a chance to cause the disease again.

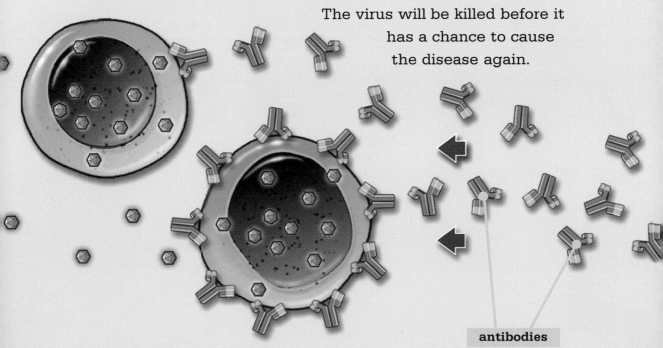

antibodies

People also have a way to get immunity without having a disease. It's called a vaccine.

Vaccines are made of **weakened or killed bacteria** or viruses that cause a particular disease. The germs aren't strong enough to make you sick. But they do trigger your immune system. It creates an army of B cells that make antibodies against those germs. In a way, vaccines fool your immune system. They send your cell defenders into action, even though the threat isn't real.

Vaccines are often given as a shot. Some are swallowed as a liquid or a pill.

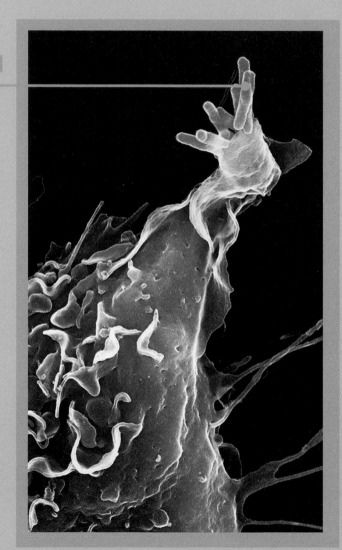

Chances are good that you've never had measles. That's because your doctor probably gave you measles vaccine when you were very young. The measles vaccine made you immune to the disease. That immunity should last for life.

So why don't we have a vaccine for every disease? Many disease-causing germs are clever invaders. Every so often, they **change some of their proteins**. It's as if they put on a mask. Vaccines can't protect us from invaders that behave this way. Your immune system doesn't recognize these germs in disguise. It treats them as new enemies. Your cell defenders mount new attacks from scratch.

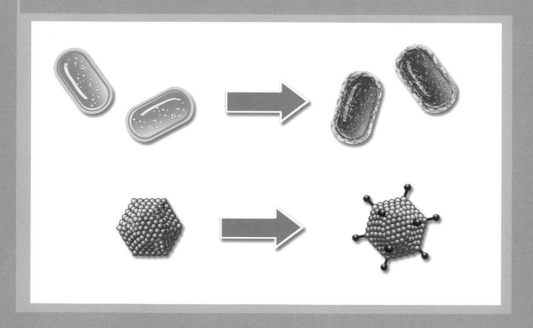

Colds are a good example. You have probably had lots of colds in your life. That's because the **viruses that cause colds** are constantly changing. Have you ever gotten over a cold, just to come down with another one? That happened because the second virus wasn't identical to the first. It was just different enough that your cell defenders didn't recognize it. And so you got a runny nose and a sore throat all over again while your cell defenders mounted another attack.

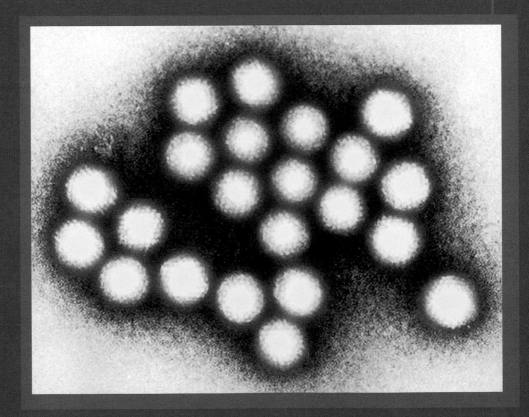

But the important thing is . . . you got better. Your immune system fought another battle and won.

Most of the time, you don't even realize that your neutrophils, macrophages, T cells, and B cells are there. But they are always standing guard. Every minute of every day, these wonderful groups of cells are working to protect you. They never, ever take a break.

So don't worry that you're surrounded by germs. Your daring cell defenders are ready to fight any and all invaders that manage to get inside your castle walls.

glossary

antibodies: proteins made by B cells that attach to germs and mark them as invaders

bacteria: microscopic, one-celled living things that reproduce by dividing in half

B lymphocyte (B cell): a type of white blood cell that makes antibodies

cell: the smallest unit of life. Cells are the building blocks of all living things.

cell membrane: the covering that surrounds a cell and controls what leaves and enters it

cilia: tiny, brushlike extensions of a cell's outer membrane

fever: an increase in normal body temperature due to an infection

gland: a group of cells that produces a particular substance

helper T lymphocyte (helper T cell): a type of white blood cell that helps direct the immune system's response to invasion by germs

immune system: the body system that fights infection and disease

immunity: protection from disease-causing germs that have invaded the body before

infection: an invasion of germs in the body

inflammation: heat, swelling, redness, and pain produced at the site of an infection

killer T cells: white blood cells that seek out and destroy body cells in which invaders are hiding

lymphocyte: any of several kinds of white blood cells that defend the body against invading germs

macrophage: the largest type of white blood cell. It fights infection- and disease-causing invaders.

memory B cell: a white blood cell that has made antibodies to fight a particular kind of invader and will do so again if that invader infects the body again

mucus: a slimy substance produced by cells lining the nose, mouth, and throat

neutrophil: a kind of white blood cell that is usually the first to attack invading germs

organ: a body structure made up of several different tissues that work together to carry out a particular job

proteins: chemical substances that are the building blocks of cells

pus: a gooey white substance made up of dead white cells and the bacteria they've killed

saliva: a digestive juice produced by glands in the mouth

system: a group of organs that work together to carry out a particular job in the body

tissue: a group of similar cells that work together

toxin: a poisonous substance. Many bacteria and viruses produce toxins during an infection.

vaccine: a medicine that gives a person immunity against a disease without having to get that disease

virus: very tiny germs that cause infection and disease by invading and taking over body cells

read more about the immune system

Books

Alfin, Elaine Marie. *Germ Hunter: A Story about Louis Pasteur.* Minneapolis: Carolrhoda Books, 2003.

Boudreau, Gloria. *The Immune System.* Farmington Hills, MI: Kidhaven Press, 2004.

Nye, Bill, and Kathleen W. Zoehfeld. *Bill Nye the Science Guy's Great Big Book of Tiny Germs.* New York: Hyperion Books for Children, 2005.

Romanek, Trudee. *Achoo! The Most Interesting Book You'll Ever Read about Germs.* Toronto: Kids Can Press, 2003.

Websites

HIV and AIDS
http://www.kidshealth.org/kid/health_problems/infection/hiv.html
The immune system can usually protect the body against invaders, but the HIV virus can keep it from doing its job. Learn more from this website.

How Your Immune System Works
http://www.howstuffworks.com/immune-system.htm
This Web page has lots of information about the immune system.

A Kid's Guide to Fever
http://www.kidshealth.org/kid/ill_injure/sick/fever.html
Fever is one of the ways the body fights off disease. This Web page has information on what causes fevers.

Microbe Zoo
http://commtechlab.msu.edu/sites/dlc-me/zoo/
This website has more information on the microscopic organisms that are all around you.

What Are Germs?
http://www.kidshealth.org/kid/talk/qa/germs.html
Find out about the tiny organisms that cause disease, as well as how to protect yourself from them.

index

about the author

Rebecca L. Johnson is the author of many award-winning science books for children. Her previous books include the Biomes of North America series, *The Digestive System, The Muscular System, Genetics,* and *Plate Tectonics.* Ms. Johnson lives in Sioux Falls, South Dakota.

photo acknowledgments

The photographs in this book are used with the permission of: © Dr. Gladden Willis/Visuals Unlimited/Getty Images, p. 5; © S. Lowry/Univ. Ulster/Stone/Getty Images, p. 6; © SMC Images/The Image Bank/Getty Images, pp. 7, 42; © Dr. David Phillips/Visuals Unlimited/Getty Images, p. 8; © Dennis Kunkel Microscopy, Inc., p. 12; © SPL/Photo Researchers, Inc., pp. 15, 17, 40; © Dr. David Phillips/Visuals Unlimited, p. 16; © CAMR/A. Barry Dowsett/Photo Researchers, Inc., p. 19; © Manfred Kage/Peter Arnold, Inc., p. 20; © Simko/Visuals Unlimited, p. 23; © Mediscan/Corbis, p. 28; © Alfred Pasieka/Photo Researchers, Inc., pp. 31, 37.

Front cover: © S. Lowry/Univ. Ulster/Stone/Getty Images; © Lerner Publishing Group, Inc. (illustration)